Under the Sign of the Lily

The Messianic Sophianic Age

The Messianic, Sophianic Age

I Come Soon!
I Am the Christ of God

Everything Is Communication—Gabriele

God-Father—The Eternal Word

*The Eternal Word,
The One God, the Free Spirit,
speaks through Gabriele,
as through all the prophets of God—
Abraham, Job, Moses, Elijah, Isaiah,
Jesus of Nazareth,
the Christ of God*

*The Messianic,
Sophianic Age*

*I Come Soon!
I Am the Christ of God*

*Everything Is Communication—
Gabriele*

*God-Father—
The Eternal Word*

"I Come Soon!
I Am the Christ of God"

"Everythings Is Communication—Gabriele"

"God-Father—The Eternal Word"

1st Edition November, 2021
©Gabriele-Verlag Das Wort GmbH
Max-Braun-Str. 2, 97828 Marktheidenfeld
www.gabriele-verlag.com
www.gabriele-publishing-house.com

Original German Title:

„Ich komme bald!
Ich Bin der Christus Gottes"

„Alles ist Kommunikation—Gabriele"

„Gott-Vater—Das Ewige Wort"

The German edition is the work of reference for all
questions regarding the meaning of the contents.

Translation authorized by:
Gabriele-Verlag Das Wort GmbH

All Rights Reserved
Order No. S 192en

Printed by: KlarDruck GmH, Markheidenfeld, Germany

ISBN 978-3-96446-229-9

Contents

I Come Soon!
I Am the Christ of God

*Christ, the Son of God and Co-Regent of
the Kingdom of God, Gave a Revelation
in March 2019 through the Prophetess and
Emissary of God, Gabriele* 7

Everything Is Communication—Gabriele

*Spiritual-Divine Teachings by Gabriele,
the Prophetess and Emissary of God,
Given in March 2019* 59

God-Father—The Eternal Word

*God-Father, the Eternal All-One,
Gave a Revelation in March 2019 through
His Prophetess and Emissary Gabriele* 101

I Come Soon!
I Am
the Christ of God

*Christ, the Son of God
and Co-Regent of the Kingdom of God,
Gave a Revelation in March 2019
through the
Prophetess and Emissary of God,
Gabriele*

The Messianic, Sophianic Age

I Come Soon!
I Am the Christ of God

Jesus of Nazareth, the incarnated Christ, was asked 2000 years ago by His apostles and disciples:

"When will You come in power and glory?"

I answered: "I come soon."

2000 years on Earth have passed. Few people think about the fact that in eternity 2000 years mean little, if not to say, nothing. Eternity has neither past nor future. Eternity is simply eternal, without time and space.

Eternity is the eternal law of eternity.

It is God, the Eternal, from Order to Meekness, also called Mercy. It is the seven basic powers of the eternal Being.

The Being is the Kingdom of God. The primordial principle God, the spiritual-atomic power of the Light-Ether, is the primordial Love and primordial Wisdom. From this primordial Being, primordial Love and primordial Wisdom, emerged the eon-orbits of the seven basic powers, in each of which the other basic powers are respectively contained as further eons.

All seven times seven eons orbit the center of the Being, the Sanctum of God, and receive the creating and drawing power for their further course in the eternal Being. All Being receives the inexhaustible Light-Ether from the center of the Being, from the Sanctum of God.

In Himself, the primordial Spirit, God, beheld His work of creation, the All-Being. In Himself, in the flowing Light-Ether, He beheld His works and placed them in His seven basic powers. It is the law of unity, of the love for God and neighbor.

The image of creating and drawing, God, the primordial Love and primordial Wisdom, is the entirety in the image of creating and drawing in the Light-Ether. From this, in the rhythm of creating and drawing, emerged the first seven entities, the sons of heaven, the bearers of the law of the Being. The first seven sons of heaven are the first created beings. They are also called the princes or regents before the throne of God.

From the primordial image of the sons of heaven—the first manifested beings of creation, the Cherubim—the Seraphim emerged.

Cherubim and Seraphim are the stock-duals for the nation of families, that is, nation of children, for the life in the Father-Mother-Being.

In this orbit of drawing and creating of the primordial God, the Kingdom of God continued to expand. Four planes of evolution, the same as planes of development, are integrated in the Kingdom of God. The four planes of development are the "Let there be" for the nation of children.

The total picture of the Being comes forth from the primordial Love and the primordial Wisdom. In this course of the law, the

Father-Mother-God is the giving, pulsating life, which is unity, the Being in the Being, the Kingdom of God.

The first son, the Co-Regent of the Kingdom of God, emerged from the dual principle of the Father-Mother-Being.

With the desire of several spirit beings to fashion creation differently than as the primordial Spirit, God, had beheld it, the Fall began.

For the repatriation of the Fall, the Co-Regent of the Kingdom of God, the first Son in the Father-Mother-Being, assumed the task of turning a part of His inheritance as Co-Regent into the energy of Redemption for the fallen children of God, as a protection for the core of being in every soul, the essence of the Kingdom of God.

The times of times passed, and I appeared in Jesus of Nazareth as the Announced One.

The Co-Regent of the Kingdom of God, who I Am, incarnated in Jesus of Nazareth. From the first hour as a human child, the wave of annihilation of the adversary from below pursued Me, to destroy every undertaking from above, from the Kingdom of God.

It was similar for the princes of heaven, who incarnated in a human body in times of times, as it was for Me as Jesus of Nazareth. All who brought the message from the Kingdom of God, in order to give an understanding of their eternal being to willing and seeking people, were persecuted and mistreated accordingly—often, all the way to death.

Whether it was the eternal word through the prophets of God or through Me as Jesus of Nazareth, the message from the Kingdom of God was always the same: God is the love for God and neighbor.

In My mission as Jesus of Nazareth, was an additional process of becoming that went far beyond the message of the prophets of God.

My additional mission as the Son of God in Jesus of Nazareth was the liberation of souls and ensouled human beings from the wheel of reincarnation, in order to release and free them from all that the opposing forces—the father from below, as I called the adversary of God—had thought up to bind them.

According to the will of the adversary, the wheel of re-embodiment, of reincarnation, should be the wheel of annihilation of the soul bodies, and thus, bring about the dissolution of God's creation.

Through the martyrdom, the Deed of Redemption on the cross, the wheel of reincarnation takes up only those souls, which, as human beings, knowingly, that is, without hesitation, go against the law of love for God and neighbor, against the absolute, divine law of freedom that every soul bears in itself. It is the Ten Commandments of God and the Sermon on the Mount of Jesus, the Christ—the essence of the love for God and neighbor.

The one who wants to, and does, release himself from the wheel of reincarnation takes the Ten Commandments of God through Moses and the teachings in the Sermon on the Mount seriously, just as they were taught.

The Ten Commandments of God and the Sermon on the Mount are steps of the law to the Kingdom of God, to the Father-Mother-God. It is the path of liberation from binding and reincarnation. The cross on Golgotha without the corpus is the sign of liberation from the binding wheel of reincarnation.

The simple, yet rich in content words, *"It is finished, it is done—Father, in Your hands is My Spirit,"* reveal that the mission of Jesus of Nazareth is fulfilled.

Time passes—but not eternity.

What are 2000 years in the spirit of eternity?

The prophets and prophetesses of God and many God-conscious men and women prepared My coming as Jesus of Nazareth and, at the same time, built up the cosmic radiation for the New Age, the New Era, toward the Kingdom of Peace of the Christ of God, of the spiritual Messiah.

Through the prophet Isaiah, God, the Eternal, introduced the turn of time. Although I, the Son of God, was not yet incarnated in Jesus of Nazareth and the "It is finished, it is done" had to still take place, the Eternal announced it through Isaiah, and prepared the spiritual-divine chronicle for it.

The Prince of Wisdom, the third basic power before God's throne, once in Isaiah, prepared the divine atmosphere, in order to have the eternal word after Jesus of Nazareth become what is now announced: "I, Christ, come soon."

As revealed:

The messianic, sophianic age, the Christ Age, the New Era, was prepared by the prophet Isaiah and carried into the world by further righteous men and women. Thus, My coming has been prepared long since, and the atmospheric Christ-chronicle for the New Era was laid out, the foundation for the Kingdom of Peace of Jesus, the Christ.

The estrangement from God is defeated.

The system of "divide, bind and rule" that is world-oriented, will very gradually come to an end.

The Eternal in Me, the Christ, gives the directive in this world:

My Son, the Christ of God, has prevailed!

The powerful, with their prognoses of power and the solidarity of church and state, are merely temporary.

God, the Eternal, the law of freedom, does not have the time of human beings. Therefore, it is also not comprehensible to human beings, when this world-oriented time comes to an end. Although the end is still conditioned by time, it is already visible.

Humankind itself provides the signs for when this world and this time come to an end.

Silently and without much ado, the New Era unfolds, the messianic, sophianic age under the sign of the lily, Sophia—"I, Christ, come soon."

I, Christ, do not come as a human being. I appear as the spiritual Messiah, the Liberator, and as the King of the Kingdom of Peace that is lighting up and that will be ushered in by the New Era.

Sophia, the divine Wisdom, holds My throne ready, which is building up more and more in the Christ-of-God atmosphere. I will sit on the Christ-Sophia throne and reign according to the law of the All-One, which is the love for God and neighbor.

It is as it is:

The present and future atmospheric events bear the signs of the passing of this time and of the coming times. From generation to generation, the times will become more light-filled. In the course of these times of transformation, the times to come will no longer be determined by people who are bound by religious constraints. It will be an ongoing cosmic "peeling" process. With the atmospheric layers, it will take place in a similar way as with an onion. The entities of God, His law-guardians, carry out the cosmic peeling process.

Among other things, the task of the divine Wisdom is to prepare the souls in the purification planes for God, the Eternal, and to show ensouled people the path into the life that is the love for God and neighbor.

The doors and gates into the kingdom, into the Kingdom of Heaven, stand open. On this Earth, one can read and also hear about the path to there in the *Sophia Library* and in the pearl from the Sanctum of God, the *Tent of God* in the *Ark of the Covenant of the Free Spirit* for all the people of all the nations of this Earth.

The eternal word of the All-One God is set there; it comes to souls and human beings by way of the Christ of God chronicle, the Christ atmosphere, and by way of the prism suns of the Sanctum. In the *Tent of God* and in the *Sophia Library* is largely written what was announced by the prophetesses and prophets of God.

I repeat: It is set by the prince, the Cherub of the eternal Wisdom, once in the prophet Isaiah, who brought it in revelation through the prophetess of God, Gabriele, for the New Era that is building up.

Come, Oh come, all here, from all the nations of the Earth, and immerse yourselves in the word of the Eternal God, which is also My message, that of the Christ of God!

For thousands of years, My coming, the life in the Spirit of God, was announced by the prophets of God. Again and again, My coming was announced.

It is not a new announcement:

"I, the spiritual Messiah, come soon."

After My life on Earth in Jesus of Nazareth, centuries upon centuries went by. My coming as the spiritual Messiah was revealed to many enlightened men and women. Over the course of these times, the messianic, sophianic age, the New Era, the building of the New Jerusalem, was very gradually revealed.

Despite all resistance from the forces of the opposition, from the Kingdom of God a mighty time was introduced, the New Age, the coming of the spiritual Messiah, of the Christ of God, who I Am.

The old fever of belonging to a religion still holds many people under its spell.

With the centuries-old feverish compulsion, the compulsion of religion, many people still accept everything as it was forced on them from childhood on by the religious leaders of various religious castes.

I, Christ, once in Jesus of Nazareth, did not found a religion and appointed no religious leaders—like priests, pastors, bishops, cardinals—nor did I choose any so-called holy fathers. I did not advocate any churches and temples.

How could I! I taught that every soul and every ensouled human being are themselves the temple in which God, the life, dwells.

In Jesus of Nazareth I praised God, the omnipresent power, the eternal Spirit, the life in Me, in human beings and souls, in the nature kingdoms, in the entire universe, the All, for God, the Eternal, is the All-One Free Spirit, the omnipresent life.

In many so-called religious ideologies, it is said that I, Jesus of Nazareth, was a prophet, which is ultimately true. In all the prophets of God, divine beings were incarnated, in order to show the people, in their respective time and language, the way to the life and to prepare the coming of the spiritual Messiah.

However, at all times and into this time, humankind has barely grasped, and grasps, what the messengers of God, the prophets of God, proclaimed and proclaim. And in this time, most religious believers do not understand that I, the Christ of God, once in Jesus of Nazareth, announced My coming, and this, over and over again, until the culmination point is reached, the coming of the spiritual Messiah.

As Jesus of Nazareth, I taught the law of life, which is the way to the eternal Father's house, to the eternal dwellings that are waiting for purified, that is, cleansed, souls.

In its religious compulsions, humankind did not, and does not listen to the prophets sent by God. Just as little, did they listen to the proclaimer of God, the prophet Jesus of Nazareth, the Son of Man, who was the embodiment of the Son of God in the human being Jesus.

Into the present time, many people still let themselves be fettered to religious constraints, to an acrobatics of faith surrounding the little child of Bethlehem. They believe in, and adhere to crucifixes and bind themselves to ecclesiastical sacral institutions, which have incorporated My Name—Christ, the Son of God—into their numerical code, the same as a deposit slip, in order to do business with My Name. Their "dignitaries in cassocks," too, are the means and the end for this.

Through the power of the All-Just One, the prophets of God and all faithful men and women, including Me, the Christ, have cut off the adversary's taproot, his most covetous desire: the dissolution of the creation of Being.

The sacrifice of Jesus of Nazareth on the cross was not the sacrifice of suffering for human beings and souls, but for overcoming death through resurrection in the love for God and neighbor, by which the dissolution of souls and the dissolution of the primordial-eternal creation was prevented.

The cross without the corpus, without the corpse of Jesus, is the sign and the way into the Father's house. Likewise, it is also the sign of resurrection to the eternal life, to the eternal Being.

I Christ, Am the resurrection and the life. I come soon.

Deep in the core of being of each soul is the spark of life, which I Am in God, the Eternal.

Therefore, I Am the way and, for each soul, the resurrection to the true life, which is inviolable.

I repeat:

Thde father from below, the adversary, has lost, although he has had the cross with the corpus positioned for 2000 years.

My mission is fulfilled. The Christ of God, the Son of the All-Highest, not only resurrected and returned to the Eternal Father, but He also brought to all souls the resurrection to the true life, no matter to which religious faith the ensouled human being still belongs.

Religions, regardless of the religious orientation they profess, are a means to an end for the respective rulers of a nation.

No matter what religions and state coffers demand, religion is religion, state is state, both are part of the veil that still lies over the people.

As revealed:

The atmosphere of the Christ of God is established, it stands because of the prophets and prophetesses of God, the many men and women who are faithful to God, and because of the fulfilled task of the Son of God, the Christ of God.

I come soon!

The prophets and prophetesses of God and all righteous men and women are the escort of the spiritual Messiah. They have made their contribution to the liberation of all souls and ensouled human beings and to the liberation of the animals, of the entire Mother Earth.

The cosmoses of the Fall, which were once inhabited by the Fall-beings, will also very gradually be led back into the eternal law of the Kingdom of God. In this connection, the purified souls will also return to the eternal Father's house, as beings of the Being. Many souls and people are of the opinion that this is still a long way off, but what are 1000 years in eternity?

My call resounds in all the cosmoses of the Fall. It is directed to souls and to the ensouled human beings on the Earth:

Awaken! I, Christ, the spiritual Messiah, come soon.

Together with the Wisdom out of God, the third basic power before the throne of God, I, the Christ of God, fetch home everything that lets itself be taken home, into the eternal Kingdom of Peace.

For understanding, may the meaning of the messianic, sophianic age be repeated once more: A new heaven and a new Earth.

Cherubim and Seraphim, in accord with the Son of God, fetch home and, at the same time, retrieve what is outside the Wall of Light of the eternal Being, the Kingdom of God.

Despite the fact that some beings turned away from God with the compulsive thought of being able to do everything better than the Creator of the All—from which polytheism arose—everything has been accomplished by the All-One Free Spirit, the eternal law of the love for God and neighbor.

The primordial-eternal law has no violence in it. Consequently, God, the Eternal, is not a tyrant, but solely the law of love for God and neighbor.

The true God is not an advocate of violence, not a warmonger or weapons expert or a gravedigger. He is exclusively the way to life, the law of the love for God and neighbor.

All the prophets of God, all God-filled men and women rejected the murder of human beings and animals. They taught the One true God, the commandment of unity, which is the love for God and neighbor.

People who feel bound to time and space seldom look any deeper. Words such as "this will take a long time" also suggest the play on words of a "short time."

Verily, the times of times change in eternity. Time and space, a "long time" or a "short time" belong to the transience, for the light-reflexes in the universes will increase, indicating what has been announced: I come soon.

I come in the Spirit of My Father, who is also the Father of every soul and of every ensouled human being.

If the human being would have the deep and free belief that he has a soul and that the cleansed soul will again become a heavenly being, a spirit being, then soul and person would have taken a large step on the path to the eternal One God and Father, who is in heaven and who works through His prophets and prophetesses and through enlightened people.

The Spirit of truth moves people in all the nations of this Earth to follow the path to Him, who is the law of the unalterable love for God and neighbor.

As Jesus of Nazareth, I taught aspects of the eternal law, as, for instance:

All that you expect from others, do this for them first!
For this is the law and the prophets.

May the one who wants to be first, be the last of all and the servant of all.

Love God who is the All-Love with all your heart and with all your soul and in all your thoughts, and then you will begin to love your neighbor as yourself.

You cannot love your neighbor and set the war machinery in motion against others. That would be hypocrisy and attempted fratricide.

I, Christ, Am the way to the true eternal love and to the eternal life; no one will come to the eternal Father except through Me.

May people be advised to make peace with their neighbor as long as they are underway with them, for no one knows when they will see one another again. For who knows what tomorrow will bring?

Your yes should be a true yes and your no, a no, for anything else can be your downfall.

No rich person will enter the Kingdom of God as long as he hoards his wealth and knows that his neighbor suffers hardship and hunger or is even dying of hunger.

The one who uses the measure of his baseness on his neighbor will be measured accordingly when the time is right.

The one who asks and fulfills the instructions of the true life can also be given to and helped.

The one who fulfills the truth—which is eternal—and acts accordingly is prudent and insightful, for he builds his spiritual house on the rock, Christ.

Thus, I taught the facets of the eternal law.

The prince of the divine Order, one of the seven law-guardians before God's throne, was incarnated in the prophet's garment of Moses. Moses brought the commandments of God, the essence of the laws of the Kingdom of God. The one who follows the commandments of God through Moses step by step, begins to fulfill the law of the All-One God more and more. As Jesus, the Christ, I taught the commandments that are connected with the Sermon on the Mount.

People who dedicate their thoughts and lives to the commandments of God and the Sermon on the Mount will never call for wars, never kill or have killed. They respect the law of peace, which is the love for God and neighbor.

As revealed, not only ensouled human beings are a part of the eternal law, the All-Law of love for God and neighbor, but also the animals and nature, the entire All-Creation—without exception.

The one who includes the commandments of God and the Sermon on the Mount in his thinking and behavior, in his path through life, understands what the words "law of incarnation" mean.

The revealed law of incarnation is part of the Fall-law—of cause and effect. It developed through the allures of "divide, bind, and rule," in which it is: one against the other. That is the Fall-thought. Due to this divisiveness, each one is responsible for his own thinking, speaking and doing.

Loneliness developed through the divisiveness.

One person takes the step-by-step path to the true life, while the other follows the path of a carefree attitude and indifference in terms of the commandments of God and the teachings of the Sermon on the Mount and makes himself his own laws. In this context, he inevitably takes upon himself the repetitions of life on Earth, the multiple incarnations. This can be a long way for a soul, from birth to birth, again and again.

The ways from birth to birth are also called the paths of expiation or the wheel of reincarnations. Via the wheel of reincarnations, of embodiments, the human paths can become very difficult, above all, when the soul that incarnates again and again as a human being, changes religions.

By changing from the teachings of gods to teachings of gods, the mystical numbers emerged, which the human beings of the present time also call numerical codes.

As already revealed:
These numerical chains, numerical codes, also called mystical numbers, emerged after the Fall of the divine beings from the Kingdom of God.

Their "gods" were already included in the cosmic hierarchies of the Fall that they created for themselves through the loan of the Light-Ether. Each so-called "god" had its Fall-number, its mystical number, which it proclaimed in order to recruit more Fall-beings. This is not surprising, because this system reaches into the present time.

In the times of times, the "gods" of the Fall built religious structures for themselves, religions with self-chosen leaders. These based themselves on charismatic people or even wrongly on the prophets of God, integrating them into their religious guilds.

Up to the present time, every religious adherent must ask himself which "god," that is, which god of religion, he worships and serves.

May it be repeated:
The eternal All-One God is the God of freedom.
Because this is so, the One, free God did not found a religion—neither through the bearers of His word, the prophets, nor through His son,

the Christ of God in Jesus of Nazareth. Religion is conditioning by numbers and dependency by numbers. Every religious adherent belongs to a Fall-number.

God, the Eternal, is the eternal law, the omnipresent Being. The Being, the omnipresent law, God, is to be seen as follows:
In the smallest is the All-Law, the whole, and in the All-Law is the smallest. God, the omnipresent Spirit, is simply omnipresent. Therefore, no religions are needed, because the eternal All-One is the All-Law, that is, the Being in all things, omnipresent.

What God, the Eternal, revealed through Me, the Christ of God in Jesus of Nazareth, is as it is:
You, the soul in the human being, are the temple of God, and God, the omnipresent Spirit, dwells in you.
When it is said: In the smallest is the All-Law, then this means that the omnipresent Spirit is also in every drop of water, in each grain of sand

and speck of dust, in all of infinity and not lastly, in every particle of the soul and in the entire cell system of an ensouled human being.

Therefore, may it be repeated again:
You are the temple of the All-One God, and God, the All-One, that is, the All-Law of the love for God and neighbor, dwells in your soul.
In many a person, the question arises: What does the All-Law, the All-Being, have to do with the teaching of reincarnation, with the law of incarnation of the soul?

I, Christ, explain: In the language of My prophetess, I, Christ, the Son of God, will choose the appropriate words that are simply characteristic of human beings, to make the deep correlations understandable when it comes to insights into the sequences of the law for journeying souls.

As already revealed, the wheel of reincarnations and the cosmic purification planes, the planetary pathways, exist from cosmos to cosmos.

God, the Eternal, the law of infinity, is the Free Spirit of the love for God and neighbor. This means that every soul and every ensouled human being has within the love for God and neighbor, the law of freedom, which means: God in you, God in infinity.

Once the ensouled human body passes on, its soul leaves the physical body. The questions of many people are: What is a soul? Where does the soul come from? What is a spiritual-divine body, a spirit being?

The soul is finer-material, that is, made of a finer substance than the substance of the material body. That is why the soul is described as finer-material and the physical body as coarse-material. The finer-material body, the soul, is in communication with the coarse-material body only in a conditional way.

Every soul is made up of a particle structure, of the very finest energetic substances, which are equal to the Light-Ether. Everything, absolutely everything, is based on energy, up to the tiniest particles, which are no longer perceived by the human eye.

The particles of the soul are similar to the particle structure of the divine body of the divine beings. The divine body of a spirit being is unburdened. In contrast, the particles of the soul of an individual human being are burdened with various inputs.

The human being talks about matter. In reality, everything is energy, and everything is based on spiritual-atomic interaction. Since the divine primordial atoms are also in all the types of atoms in matter, the Spirit, God, the infinite law, is always present, that is, omnipresent.

What I, the Christ of God, describe only briefly, means that matter is nothing other than transformed-down primordial-atomic Light-Ether. All material structures are condensed spiritual-atomic energy. Every material form—

be it ever so small and hardly recognizable—is atomic energy, it is transformed-down primordial-atomic Light-Ether.

The considerable amount of primordial atomic Light-Ether, which the contrary beings received as a loan from God, the Eternal, is to be redeemed in the times of times, when it has been shown that their system of desire and wanting does not function.

The Fall-system they tried out—wanting to eliminate God, the Eternal One—has slipped so much during the times of times that one can speak of energetic explosives, among other things, also through the principle of divisiveness: one against the other, one country against the other.

The knowledge about the quantum principle could provide a certain breakdown of what breath and the breath of God signify, and what content the terms fine-material, finer-material and coarse-material have.

Despite all the efforts regarding this, the statement remains: Everything is primordial-atomic Light-Energy.

The times of times are approaching the end-time.

What the eternal God gave as a loan to the rebellious ones with their know-allness to take with them is tied to the times of times, that is, to time and space. The time for the loan is running out. Here and there, it has already run out, even though the wheel of reincarnation is still turning.

May it be repeated for understanding: The spirit being is fine-material, which means that it is compressed primordial substance of the Being, compressed primordial law of the law of love for God and neighbor. The homeland of every pure being, every spirit being, is the Kingdom of God, the life in eternal families and in the clans of the Being. It is the eternal home of the divine beings.

As revealed, the soul will be a soul for as long as its finer-material body, the particle structure, is burdened. If a soul incarnates, that is, if it becomes a human being, then it brings along the pros and cons of its particle structure, which then gradually become noticeable in the physical body.

No one other than the person himself imprints his soul. It, in turn, marks its person.

Freedom is in the law of life.

An incarnated soul can come from the wheel of reincarnations or from one of the purification planes. In the wheel of reincarnations are the souls that want to incarnate again, including heavily burdened souls that either want to expiate the condition of their souls as human beings or that want to live their imaginary world as human beings.

All degrees of consciousness—whether souls on the cosmic pathways or the ensouled people on the Earth—are free beings in every respect. Every free being decides about itself, in terms of which path it wants to follow and what this means for the being.

All souls on their pathways, also those that are in the wheel of reincarnations, see in images what might happen to them in their coming incarnation, their pros and cons.

All the pros and cons, what the soul has stored in its soul particles, is revealed to it only in allusion, and only what will come to bear for this coming incarnation. Thus, it is only the steps that it has to recognize and bear in its approaching incarnation.

As Jesus of Nazareth, I essentially taught: "Repent and clear up with your neighbor as long as you are on the way with him," which means, among other things: as long as you can still encounter one another as human beings, that is, as long as you still are in the temporal.

Once more, the repetition points out:
The wheel of reincarnations suggests that there can be a number of incarnation paths.

But after a certain period of time, the parting of ways or crossroads is shown to the soul, which people call the Redeemer-path or path of liberation. This means that a soul, depending on its burdening, can follow the path of incarnations unimaginably often.

The cycle is: Death of the physical body, exit of the soul from the physical body, re-entry into a new physical body and so on and so forth. This goes on until a certain crossroad, and then it is: out of the wheel of reincarnation and onto a certain cosmic soul-path, again determined by itself, to the next steps, which imply a higher life.

What the journeying soul encounters on each of its cosmic soul-paths, it has within itself as living pictures.

Every person feels, senses, thinks, speaks and acts in pictures, from which result these picture sequences of the soul. The pictures of the soul show, in forms, colors and respective pictorial impressions, what the soul has inflicted on itself as a human being. On its journey from cosmos to cosmos, everything that has not been cleared up comes toward the soul, everything that it had inflicted on itself as a human being and what is not remedied.

Should the pathways of the soul be ever so rough—no soul is lost. If the soul in the spheres of purification or the person in the earthly garment is willing to recognize its wrongdoings, its causes, to repent, to remedy them and no longer to commit the wrongdoing it has recognized, then the liberating Redemption, the Christ of God, is active in the very basis of the soul.

Humankind is standing at the crossroads. In the present time, it is no longer primarily the person who is called on, but his soul.

On the cross, I, Christ, the Co-Regent of the Kingdom of God, once in Jesus of Nazareth, accomplished the crossroads for souls leading out of the wheel of reincarnations, and thus abolished the possibility of the destruction of souls.

I, Christ, will make true what I promised to the people of that time as Jesus of Nazareth, which the present time will also experience:

I, Christ, come soon, the spiritual Messiah, the appearance for the New Era.
Sophia, the divine Wisdom, has announced Me and presented Me with the mild ruler crown, the wreath of light of the seven stars.

I, Christ, Am the way of the New Era and the way to the eternal All-One God, the One Father who is in heaven.

Just as all prophets and prophetesses of God and all righteous men and women in God taught the path of peace, the path of truth, which leads to the life, so did I, Christ, also teach it and still do. In Me, the Christ, they are all present life. No matter during which age and with which words—determined by the times—the path into the Father's house was, and is, taught, the word of God is the truth and is not lost.

The eternal word, the truth, cannot be obfuscated by the Baal-system of church and state, and therefore, the repetition:

The Cherub of divine Wisdom brought the word of the prophets of God into the present time through the prophetess of God of this time, through his spirit-dual, who is still in the earthly garment. The word has returned and is taught in the present time through the prophetess of the present time, in unity with the Cherub of divine Wisdom, once in Isaiah. His mission is fulfilled.

Therefore, the words of the Eternal: *"My word does not return to Me empty."* It has been fulfilled and is to be heard and read exclusively in the *Tent of God*, in the pearl from the Sanctum of God, the *Ark of the Covenant of the Free Spirit*, God.

Every soul and every ensouled human being bears within the certainty that the redeeming power of the Christ of God, who I Am, is not lost, that is, dissolved.

The Earth and all that the Planet Earth bears is subject to transformation, which means: The Earth and the entire material cosmos and all further dense cosmoses, are being spiritually structured and transformed.

It is as it is. The cross of resurrection is the fulfillment for each soul. Every soul has the freedom to decide when it will walk the path to the eternal Kingdom of God, and whether it will take this direct path or go by way of incarnations, that is, by way of becoming a human being, which means, in the wheel of reincarnations.

I repeat:
A divine being shows every soul in pictures what can come toward it during a reincarnation or what will come to it on the path to the higher Being via the finer-material cosmoses, in order to overcome it.

The times of times now indicate the transience of the times. The father from below, the adversary against God, stalked, and continues to stalk, every person who believed, and believes, in the eternal truth, in order to extinguish it.

Despite all this, the signs become visible in the times. Horse and rider, church and state, show their true face more and more. Because the divine-prophetic Spirit is not belligerent and is not religious, over the course of time, everything that is stored in the soul will come toward the soul and the person.

The disparagement of the prophets, their suffering and the murder that I, Jesus, the Christ, also had to suffer, by way of the death of agony on the cross, are signs and traces that are being uncovered more and more by the eternal truth.

People of the coming generations will see the shadow world that still exists here and there as a deterrent and draw conclusions from it, recognizing how it has fought the eternal word, to cover up the traces of eternal truth and if possible, to wipe them out.

It is becoming more and more visible: The gods of religion cannot help the people, because they are the mere extras of state and church. Solely the fulfillment of the eternal law of the Father, who is in heaven, who is goodness, love and meekness, that is, mercy, reveals to human beings and souls the way to the true life—not the fighting gods that have no value whatsoever.

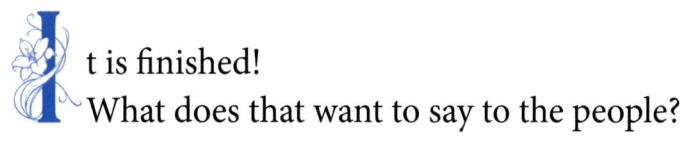t is finished!
What does that want to say to the people?

No religion can unlock this statement, but the sinner alone, himself, the person who has placed his thinking and living into the hands of the Father in heaven, who is the love for God and neighbor. Only this path leads to the life and frees soul and person from the sinful—not the dominant power of religious compulsion.

The true God is love and does not compel.
God, the Eternal, is the law of eternity that declares no war nor fights. The law of love for God and neighbor is the sign of victory, also concerning the future of humankind. It is as it is: God is eternal presence.

I repeat for the more light-filled time and for the people who want to grasp the life of the Being in its depth: The primordial-eternal law of love for God and neighbor does not strike; it does not defend itself; it does not fight against the neighbor; it does not kill and thus, it does not take to the field to conquer.

As Jesus of Nazareth, I described the perpetrator of the fight against one's neighbor as the "father from below," who was a murderer from the beginning and still practices his sacrificial cult in the still sinful world. The murderous doings started with the beginning of the Fall.

That the sinful world was this way and still is this way today—although with a certain tactic of covering things up—shows the state of this world.

What was yesterday still takes place today, as well. What the Kingdom of God has announced through all the torchbearers of yesterday, and of today, is deceitfully and subtly ascribed to the hidden system of eradication, which it serves to the people in falsified form.

The New Era brings the truth.
I Am in God, the eternal Father-Mother-God, the truth and the life.

This conveyance has the light in it:
I Am the spiritual Messiah. I come soon.

Let it be repeated:
The Eternal God, the Father from above, fetches home and retrieves what is due, for the energetic loan to the Fall-realm, to this dark world, is coming to an end. The Fall, the system of "divide, bind and rule," is defeated by the eternal law of the love for God and neighbor.

The numerical codes, as well, that went out from the religious consortium at the beginning of the Fall have worn out, although many people are still members of a religion and dependent on numbers.

No matter how the religious conglomerate and its dependents still call themselves at this time: The Fall, the law of "divide, bind and rule," is defeated.

The heavenly spark, also called the Redeemer-spark, shines in every soul. The heavenly spark is freedom, it is the way into the Kingdom of

Heaven, not the enforced baptism of water, one of the many stamps of religions.

Take note, you people in the world still shaped by many "gods":

Every soul and every ensouled person is released from the pressure of the father from below, who is a murderer and had the dissolution of souls as his goal.

No matter how this or that religion presents or calls itself: In the Spirit, God, who is freedom, there is neither religion nor coercion.

Every soul and every human being choose for themselves. The content of each individual's feelings, sensations, thoughts, words and deeds show him the way—not some kind of religious means or other.

The innermost being in every soul and in every ensouled person lives in God, who is the freedom.

May it be repeated:

Every soul and every ensouled human being are the temple of God, in which the almighty power of the love for God and neighbor dwells.

You, O human soul, are free. Choose for yourself. It is your decision.

A New Era is dawning. It is the messianic, sophianic age, the age of the lily, the New Era.

With the words of the appearance, which I, Jesus, the Christ, promised the apostles and disciples, "I come soon," a more light-filled era, the New Era, was introduced.

I Am the light of the world, the Son of the All-Highest and the Co-Regent of the Kingdom of God, once in Jesus of Nazareth. The messianic era is the era of the appearance, the era of preparation, which Sophia, the divine Wisdom, introduces. The eternal word from Abraham to Gabriele holds true in the New Era.

Once more, the eternal word of the proclaimers of God, the prophets and prophetesses of God, goes into the hearts of souls and of ensouled people, and that, with the words of the present time, spoken by the eternal All-One God and by Me, the Christ of God, and by the

Cherub of divine Wisdom through the prophetess of God for the present time—Gabriele.

As revealed:
The eternal word is being fulfilled, just as the eternal All-One revealed through His prophet Isaiah: *"My word does not return to Me empty."*

It has returned and is exclusively in the pearl from the eternal Sanctum, in the *Tent of God Among the People for All the Nations of this Earth with the Sophia Library*, to be read and listened to. That is the place where it can be heard and read, and nowhere else!

There, it is evident for the people of the New Era in the messianic, sophianic age under the sign of the lily.

Come all to Me, to the Spirit of the Christ of God; let yourselves be guided, you souls and ensouled human beings.

So it is and so will it remain.

I, Christ, repeat:

For all seeking people, the word of the Eternal is evident, written and spoken in the pearl from the eternal Sanctum, in the *Tent of God Among the People for All the Nations of this Earth, in the Ark of the Covenant of the Free Spirit.*

I Am the spiritual Messiah, the Coming One, the light for the New Era, the Christ of God, once in Jesus of Nazareth.

Everything Is Communication— Gabriele

*Spiritual-Divine Teachings
by Gabriele,
the Prophetess and Emissary of God,
Given in March 2019*

The Messianic, Sophianic Age

Everything Is Communication— Gabriele

Dear fellow people,

infinity, the All-Being, is based on evolution and communication. Our existence on Earth is based either on evolution or on degeneration. Our lines of communication are in accordance to this.

Wherever we human beings go, wherever we are, we send incessantly.

What each individual person sends out, for example, the content of his feelings, sensations, thoughts, words and actions, comes back to him, the sender—mind you: not to another person, but to him, the sender. Our house, as well, our apartment, our furnishings, our clothes, everything is energy that sends and returns to the sender, accordingly.

No matter where we live, whether we live in a city, hamlet or village, everything is based on communication, on evolution or degeneration.

Through communication, through evolution or degeneration, every person determines their process of development. The same applies to our illness, our suffering and dying, also in terms of death. Everything is communication in which the transitions lie—upward, into higher planes of consciousness, into evolution, or downward, into lower levels of communication, also called fields of communication, into degeneration.

Equally vibrating communications, whether upward or downward, form communication fields. We also call them steps of consciousness or levels of consciousness of the coarse-material existence.

This process takes place in the same way with a human being as well as a disincarnate soul.

In the Spirit of God, who is the All-Life, we human beings are free beings who decide for themselves at every moment—and this, through communication. Thus, life is communication, whether it is the path of the soul in the hereafter or the path of the human being over the Earth.

Through conscious, positive communication, soul and human being can vivify the path to the Kingdom of God, so that the soul receive the cosmic power and the physical body become more vigorous, because the consciousness expands.

Whatever we see or do not see—everything lives via communication. There is no such thing as nothing; everything is based on communication. Both the negative, the contrary, and the positive, what is willed by God, is communication. Everything is communication; everything emits; everything receives. Like attracts like.

The absolute reality of life is exclusively God, the Being.

In infinity, in the eternal Being, there is nothing dead. The true life is eternal Being and constant evolution through communication.

In reality, and in the coarse-material world, too, there is no death and nothing dead. Evolution means unfoldment, the further development upward into higher planes of communication. Degeneration means descent into lower energy fields, also called lower levels. However, everything is life; everything is consciousness and has the corresponding state of consciousness.

There is the visible and the invisible communication, whereby with invisible communication, we human beings think of dying, of death. As already mentioned, there is no dying, and no death, either. In reality, when dying, there is merely a change, to a lower or higher plane of communication, also called communication field, state of consciousness or communication road. Life as a human being on Earth as well as the life of the souls in the soul realms is communication.

I repeat:
No matter in which state of consciousness the soul or the human being is, there is solely communication, from which emerges either evolution or degeneration.

In the divine words of revelation of the All-One God and in the revelations of the Christ of God, we frequently read about the event of the Fall. These repetitions are important, to understand why it came to this degeneracy, to this turbulence in the event of creation. These turbulences, also called the Fall-event, point out what evolution and degeneration want to say to the reader.

Let us refer to the Fall-event once more. Meanwhile, we have read or heard that with the Fall-event, divine beings left the Kingdom of God, in order to prove to the primordial-eternal Creator and His creation that the Being of creation, the Kingdom of God, can be differently structured and led.

And this is how it was to be: Freedom should provide the proof.

The primordial-eternal principle of creation of the Father-Mother-God and the seven law-guardians, the Cherubim, gave the sons and daughters of the Being, who wanted to provide this proof, a considerable quantity of creation-mass to take with them on their way. It is the Light-Ether, which already had in itself the forms and colors for further primordial formation, according to the image of creation, the Kingdom of God.

Ready for their purpose and without any doubt in themselves, the Fall-beings accepted the creation quantum of Light-Ether. Although they knew that it was a loan from the Kingdom of God to enable them to prove their cause, they were firmly convinced that they would triumph over the Creator-God.

These statements are reminiscent of the people's cry of victory before war!

What came of it? Destruction, decay!

The Fall-beings first created a so-called Wall of Light around the Kingdom of God to completely disassociate themselves from the Kingdom of God. Thus, degeneration already began, for distance from your neighbor means divisiveness and therefore, degeneration.

Once they had completely left the Wall of Light behind, they fell into paroxysms of joy and believed to have already won the victory over the primordial Being.

The borrowed mass of creation, the Light-Ether, was immeasurable for them. Yet, hardly had the flush of victory diminished somewhat, and their fever of creating and drawing began, they got into disagreement with each other. Each one believed that his concept was the best.

It reminds me, Gabriele, of the Second World War.

When the Fall-beings looked deeper into the mass of creation borrowed from the Eternal God, into the Light-Ether, they realized that the mass of creation already carried images from the primordial Creation-Being, that is, specifications for further creations and drawings for the Kingdom of God. That was just right for the Fall-beings, because they did not have to create anything new anymore. They took the specifications of the pre-creations for the eternal Being, and believed that they could simply transpose them, that is, design them differently, according to their ideas and criteria.

If we look into our world and see more deeply, then we recognize the theft and abuse in terms of the Light-Ether. We human beings do not create anything out of ourselves either; we take what exists and convert it.

From the mass of creation, the borrowed Light-Ether, the Fall-beings formed their first planets, which, according to their desire and criteria, they set into motion in corresponding orbits. They made the stronger luminous planets into suns, and they assigned the other planets to the magnetic field of their so-called suns. In this way, planets orbited around a brighter so-called Central Star.

The finely flowing Light-Ether, which for them was still inexhaustible, carried their first work, which they called their cosmos. Today, after times of degeneration, humankind has only artificial celestial bodies, so-called satellites, as self-created works. The Fall-beings did not yet realize that their works took on a lower degree of vibration, just as themselves, who were once fine-material beings. That is degeneration.

In paroxysms of joy, they began further transformations from the borrowed spiritual-atomic Light-Ether. They fashioned their cosmoses. Right at the beginning of their works, the division into systems began.

The Fall-experts—this is what I want to call them—had their ideas. What they overlooked, however, was the fact that they always used only the divine pre-creation images before the evolution into the primordial creation as matrixes and incorporated them into their concepts. The first transformations, the same as reformations, were transformed down into ever-coarser vibrations. The borrowed primordial material, the Light-Ether, the fine-material, became coarse-material. Today we take this degeneration as a given.

They themselves, the Fall-experts, hardly noticed this, although admonitions and indications came from the Kingdom of God again and again. During the course of the times of the Fall, the law-princes, the Cherubim, the co-founders of the Kingdom of God, also came to the Fall-worlds to enlighten them and enable them to turn back to the Kingdom of God.

The Fall-beings ridiculed any helping hand from the Kingdom of God and were very annoyed by these troublemakers, the Cherubim, which they also expressed with corresponding acts of violence. They continued to give expression to their works, because there seemed to be enough creation mass for all the fallen beings.

The Fall-experts were in disagreement and argued with each other, because each thought they knew better than the other. Since the borrowed Light-Ether seemed inexhaustible to them, they hardly noticed that they were losing insight into the eternal Being. They saw that their created planetary systems functioned and continued. Today, the Earth-dweller hopes that the satellites he has launched will function.

With the continual violation of the law of God, another Fall-cosmos emerged, which in its structure, was denser in energy than the other one, so that, with their degree of density, the Fall-beings could see only their own density-creations. This transformation from the Light-Ether proved to be a degeneration. It became dark around them. What was previously for them farsightedness and insight into the Light-Ether creations of the Being, was now no longer self-evident. As if blind, they felt their way to the cosmoses and energies of Light-Ether lying before them. Now it became more difficult. Either they had to be satisfied with their lot and continue like this, or they had to turn back, which means to let go of their fever of creating and drawing, and transform back up again their already recognized works of the Fall.

What is it like in our time? As known, we human beings carry on until so-called blows of fate prompt the person to reflect.

Many of the rebellious beings continued. I would like to pause for a moment with the word "many," because not all Fall-beings were struck with the fever of blindness. Some beings recognized the senselessness of it and remained behind. The other set of the Fall continued.

The systems condensed. The brothers and sisters of the Fall indeed still saw their desires for the future, which they could also still fulfill, but the insight and the farsightedness became more and more limited. This is simply called degeneration. The consciousness of the Fall brothers and sisters became narrower, and the obtuseness grew, because their view was only limited. The Fall had its measure and its weight. The density of the Fall increased.

Today's experts are of the opinion that things would get better in the near future or in future times. People have so many contingencies and assume that things will get better. But it stays the same: "One assumes"—and continues to degenerate.

What is revealed in the present time about the Fall from the divine-spiritual knowledge, everything that we read and hear, is merely a small glimpse, because the entire system of the Fall can never be described with human words.

Everything we humans see, or also what we do not see, is spiritual-atomic Light-Ether, albeit so misused, condensed and transformed down, that the human being talks about matter—and people accept it as it seems and yet is not, because in its origin everything is simply Light-Ether.

If even more words were made about an expiring system, this would merely bring out an exorbitant, truly indescribable confusion about what was built up in the times of times, and has now reached the depths of its Fall, its density. It cannot go any lower, only the dissolution of the world disaster would be left.

The total dissolution of the Being was prevented by Jesus, the Christ, the Co-Regent of the Kingdom of God, of the Being, and thus made impossible.

It is finished.

Dear fellow people, during the course of the description on the Fall-system, it was also reported about beings who recognized the wrong path shortly before the beginning of the deepest degeneration and therefore, no longer followed the Fall-system. Nonetheless, at the beginning of the Fall, they had accepted the mystical numbers from the respective Fall-system, through which they are bound.

The mystical numbers are conditioned by the Fall. This means that every Fall-being that has participated in the effort to win the victory against God, the All-One, shares the responsibility for the Fall-event. By accepting the mystical numbers, the Fall-beings that remained behind had ultimately shown the desire and the will to help dissolve the primordial creation. Even if they no longer actively participated in the middle of the downfall, they still share the responsibility for it, and be it only until the beginning of the degeneration. Even if they have again turned to the eternal Being, the

Kingdom of God, nonetheless, they still carry in their bodies the mystical number to below, that needs to be dissolved. Each of these beings strives to transform upward its part in the Fall-event. In this awareness, to bring back everything that has fallen, they serve in the work of the Christ of God, in the homebringing of their brothers and sisters and in the transformation of the condensed system, which is called matter.

The degeneration of humankind, the loss of knowledge about the why and how so, can be compared to a blindfold. We can also define it with the word, change of consciousness or state of consciousness or term it the deepest degeneration or even assign it to the mystical Fall-code.

The mystical numbers remind us of the human numerical code, of a conditional cycle of pros and cons—of the DNA code, which contains the specifications for the formation of the human body, up to digitized identity cards, which signal membership in certain human groups. This also reminds us of the baptism of a child; in the end, the child is received, that is, integrated, into a certain religious system.

As already revealed by the divine, according to its origin, the being of the Fall was the finest material, that is, fine-material. It was the compressed law from the primordial Being, the Light-Ether.

Dear fellow people, the path again leads to there. It is called change and transformation to the origin of the Being, of the pure creation of Being, which is the Light-Ether that became form. The Light-Ether, also called spiritual-atomic Light-Ether, was and is the loan to the so-called brothers and sisters of the Fall. What we denote as finer-material or transformed down, but also what we call coarse-material matter, is nothing other than transformed down Light-Ether.

The process of becoming, from fine-material being to finer-material being all the way to becoming a human being is always the transformation of the Light-Ether and the degeneration. However, in its inmost being, everything is spiritual-atomic Light-Ether.

In the Light-Ether is the image for further creations.

The Light-Ether contains suns and dwelling planets, as well as the divine families, the clans, the nature kingdoms, animals, all in all, the Being in the Being, and not lastly, the streaming, finely-flowing Being, which, in turn, is Light-Ether, the law of the Being, which bears within all forms, colors, symphonies and developments, the same as powers of unfoldment, that is, evolution.

If we consider that seven dimensions, that is, the fine-material realm of the Being, were transformed down to three dimensions, the question then arises, whether the three dimensions are merely an assumption, until the chess pieces are again transposed?

Anyone who examines the history of humankind as far as possible and analytically observes the current excesses of human presumption, recognizes that the so-called progress of humankind is going on crutches, because what is today can no longer be there tomorrow. Whether it is wind power or nuclear power or satellites or the Internet or the most modern arsenals of weapons or the major corporations or world trade—all in all, it must be questioned, also in respect to the following: What if the electricity fails, if storms rage, if too much or too little rain or snow falls, if power plants fail, or even if bacteria and viruses find their way to people via the test laboratories, or if the food supply collapses even in the so-called affluent countries, because erosion and poor harvests increase more and more, or if the worldwide shortage of drinking water inevitably leads to conflicts, and so on and so forth—what then?

Basically, humankind, above all science, the state and not lastly, the religions, ought to capitulate and confess that it is over with this humankind.

The world as such is far from evolution or transformation; not even a further degeneration is still possible, unless it be artificially created people and, if it were possible according to a "scientific" elixir, an artificial nature. However, what would mammals, which also include human beings, then live on?

The indifference speaks: "The dying of insects, too, is simply as it is; the flowers can be pollinated by other means." The arrogance and ignorance of humankind toward nature is boundless; nature will teach it otherwise.

With the conquest of space, that is also such a thing. Although the attempts in this regard are many-sided, it will eventually be: earth to earth. Even if quantum decoding should provide certain information, it still means: Soon there will be no more bread for large parts of humankind and soon there will be little or no clean drinking water, or even no water at all.

To where is the vehicle called "progress" heading? As they say: downhill. At some point it will stop. At some point, the vehicle will rot away. The whole process can also be termed dying.

Indeed, death, according to many, is always the end. Yet, with the death of humankind and this world, the planet Earth will not die. It will continue to revolve around the sun and will feel much freer and somewhat lighter. In the coming times, the planet Earth will move around a solar system with a different field of communication, in which all planets are included.

Who determines the orbits of the planets around the corresponding suns?

Generally, it is said: the law of gravitation.

Where does the law of gravitation come from?

Science gives explanations. Their technical language is so wordy and detailed that the not wealthy, simple person merely nods his head and says: "Science knows."

The divine Wisdom explains little about this. It says: Everything is based on energy, on atomic structure, and everything is structured spiritual-atomic Light-Ether. All heavenly bodies move in a sea of Light-Ether and move in their orbits in this sea, even if—for lack of knowledge—science calls the transformed-down Light-Ether antimatter.

Everything, absolutely everything, is spiritual-atomic Light-Ether.

All outer space is a sea of Light-Ether.

The universe that is visible to us human beings is nothing other than transformed-down Light-Ether.

The human body also developed in such a similar sea of Light-Ether, because the Light-Ether is the creating and drawing energy of the Being. The Light-Ether contains matrixes upon matrixes. The matrixes contain, in turn, fine-material minerals of all kinds, plants and trees, as well as all animal species, and not lastly, the ethereal divine Being that became form—all of it is spirit out of the Spirit of God, the eternal primordial energy, the Light-Ether.

If we speak about the material cosmos, then we should assume that it is nothing other than Light-Ether, which the Fall-beings transformed down from finer cosmoses into coarser cosmoses. The finer-material cosmoses do not have the density of the coarse-material cosmos, of matter.

All planets of all cosmoses are embedded in a finer substance. It is a distinctly transformed-down Light-Ether, for there is nothing else than spiritual-atomic Light-Ether. As revealed: The rebellious brothers and sisters from the Kingdom of God received from the eternal kingdom exclusively Light-Ether to take with them, a loan from the Creator. It was, and is, Light-Ether.

I repeat:

In the primordial substance Light-Ether, are human beings, animals, plants and minerals of all kinds. This contains the fine-material primordial matrixes for the further development of the fine-material Being. Light-Ether is thus fine-material substance, light energy, out of which coarse materiality developed.

The entire Fall-system came out of the sea of Light-Ether.

The sea became a soft mass; we would say: water. Density, the matter of today, came from the sea.

Much can be said about the emergence of the material universe and of humankind. Today, it can only be said about this: deepest degeneration. This had its beginning. The end is preprogrammed.

The Alpha is the primordial creation; the Omega is the end of the Fall.

In the Omega is the transformation and the transformation up to the primordial Being.

The Creator of the primordial Being has prevailed.

HE is the victor. He is the primordial-eternal life.

The eternal life is fine-material and the eternal Kingdom of God is fine-material, eternally.

Dear fellow people, Jesus of Nazareth, the Christ of God, gave a mighty promise to His own. His words essentially say: *"I come soon."*

What are 2000 years, when the entire Fall-event is mentioned as "in the times of times"?

Jesus, the Christ, makes true what He promised as Jesus of Nazareth. Once more, the Christ of God has announced His coming in the messianic, sophianic age of the lily. His words through His prophetess are: *"I, Christ, Am the resurrection and the life; I come soon."*

People in His Spirit, who are building the Kingdom of Peace of Jesus, the Christ, together, and who, with many brothers and sisters in the messianic, sophianic age, are aligning their life to higher values, also take part in prayer, which ushers in a New Era.

Prayer means the progressive unfoldment of a higher life. In the messianic, sophianic age under the sign of the lily, prayer means: communication. In the future, prayers will be the communication of unity.

People in the Spirit of the Christ of God, of the spiritual Messiah, bring their prayers into connection with nature. For example, a leaf that just now falls from a tree and catches our eye can tell us more than a person whom we meet—as we say—by chance. Our sense of sight has stimulated us to communicate with the leaf. Because our eye fell on it, it has a message for us. The prayer that is communication can help us to understand ourselves better.

Communicative prayers should always have a higher goal. The goal of a person in the messianic, sophianic age should be a consciously meaningful life that strives for higher spiritual values.

The true life means living in the All-power of God. That should be our aspiration.

Our five senses are senses of perception. Everything we see or do not see is based on communication. What we see and what we hear always wants to convey something to us. What we smell, taste and touch also has a message in it. The sensory perception can show us our state of consciousness. From this, we can conclude what is due, what we could remedy, in order to develop ourselves further. Our present state of consciousness can show us our further way, which we could take in order to draw closer to the life in the very basis of our soul.

If we want to live a somewhat ethical and moral life, then we should orient ourselves to the Ten Commandments of God and to the teachings of Jesus of Nazareth that are composed in His Sermon on the Mount. There is no need of religion for this. God, the Eternal, did not found any religions; nor did Jesus of Nazareth.

For me, there is solely the word of the All, which God is through His prophets, and the word of Jesus, the Christ.

Honesty to ourselves shows the balancing act, either upward or downward, there is nothing in between. Let us keep reminding ourselves that the contents of our five components—feelings, sensations, thoughts, words and actions—have an effect on our five senses as well, primarily on our senses of sight and hearing. Usually, we hardly notice that with certain emotional receptors, for example, the sense of sight or hearing, we also program the contents of the other senses. If we do not take ourselves to task, our feelings often wander around. This shapes our whole behavior.

What we express, that is, what we pass on with words and also through our behavior and gestures, can also be influenced from without. Thereby, our emotional level is of central importance.

Without self-control, images that are momentarily meaningless to us and seem to be like random thoughts can be introduced into our sensations from without. Such—as we say—coincidences, can be transmitted to us from without, in order to determine us, to manipulate us and, under certain circumstances, to press us into a way of looking at things that does not correspond to our momentary will and thinking. Therefore, it is important to be with ourselves and to make use of our days and to allow only the images that are a guide for our further spiritual development.

Focusing also helps us to do this. To focus means to direct our current state of consciousness on the image that moves us, or on the thoughts that we cannot easily switch off. In this way, we can expand our consciousness through self-recognition and conscious living, in order to find the path that means all-conscious living.

Our sensory perception, which activates our thoughts, can therefore be of importance to us, if we want.

Whatever comes to mind by chance may have a message for us. Suddenly, we think of conversations with certain people, or we have childhood memories and much more.

We learn by returning to our level of feeling and focusing on what the images or memories, which are also stored in images, show us, that is, what they want to tell us. By focusing, our feelings are stimulated, certain nerve pathways and, depending on what we are dealing with, our nerve plexus, making our memories more active and meaningful.

Our whole body is interspersed with nerves. Certain nerves bring a picture or some pictures in us into action, into vibration. These movements can contain messages for us. They do not necessarily have to be memories. They can also be just a picture, or it can be occurrences, even vague, incomprehensible memories from previous incarnations. Such moments of images or memories may want to draw our attention to the fact that something similar also exists in the present, for instance, a disagreeable situation with certain people, possible quarrels in the family or with colleagues at work. What stirs our nerves can hold a message. In every situation we can learn to recognize ourselves—also by focusing.

Nothing happens by chance: Even if we do not want to talk about certain feelings and thoughts with certain people, it is not a coincidence. Everything wants to tell us something.

Infinity consists of communication and fields of communication, including the material cosmos with the planet Earth and with everything that lives on it, in it and above it. Every planet in our solar system carries unimaginable messages addressed to souls and ensouled human beings.

Many a one does not believe in the existence of a soul. Nevertheless, we are a part of the universe.

I believe in reincarnation. It is a key to much that is questioned. Should you not believe in reincarnation, you could think about energy. As we know, no energy is lost, whether it is positive or negative energy. Through energy we send, and through energy we receive. According to the cosmic law of attraction this means: Every human being is a sender and receiver. What we send out, the positive as well as the negative, comes back to us.

What do we send out?

What do we take in? And with what do we burden or absolve ourselves?

If no energy is lost, then where does my part of this energy go when I die, and where will this part be when I am deceased? To what other substance will my part of energy belong then? However, if we believe that the energy is maintained, then we also believe in a finer-material body, which we generally call the soul.

For understanding: The difference between the divine being that is preparing for incarnation and a soul that through its shell, its person, has inflicted a burden on itself, is that the divine being has voluntarily covered itself with corresponding energies from the purification planes, as opposed to a soul that has inflicted sinfulness upon itself, through its human body. In this case, the person has burdened his soul with his transgressions. The burdens are always the result of the contents of the five components.

We humans do not live without danger. As stated, everything is based on communication, which means that like is in communication with like. Everything is based on energy, and like energy attracts, in turn, like energy. Since we know that no energy is lost, we are constantly exposed to the radiation that is similar to the radiation we emit, both the radiation on the Earth and the radiation in the Earth, as well as what radiates above the Earth. Thus, every human being is more or less a prisoner of his own radiation potential.

If that is as it is, then what we put into the Earth will also radiate, including what we dig under and bury, but also what is above the Earth, such as the satellites that we human beings send into the atmosphere.

Surely many of us can affirm this, but how is it if we now hear that the dead bodies that we entrust to the earth also radiate, even if they are burned, since ashes also radiate? Embalmed bodies radiate, as well, but also the dead bones of people who died hundreds of years ago and of which not all are uniformly earth substance.

Everything that is not pure earth substance has corresponding communication fields in the Earth, and beyond that, in the heavenly bodies, to which our solar system also belongs. From this, the pathways of the souls to the corresponding purification planets develop. Everything that is not pure earth substance radiates on and in the Earth and enters into communication with human beings, and if possible, also with souls, which radiate similarly.

Each radiation is connected, and thus, in communication, with equally vibrating energy. Similar image frequencies can also form fields of communication that people can additionally reinforce and expand with thoughts such as fears or accusations. Like always attracts like and communicates with like.

Medications are also energies that communicate with a similar or even the same symptoms. If the communication field of a disease is disturbed, it can lead to changes that are not good, because like always affects like.

Everything is based on communication, on evolution or on degeneration.

The course of our solar system also has a meaning that is rich in content. Our days are determined by the mornings, afternoons and evenings, and also by the night.

Broadly speaking, we are cosmic beings. Our days, the seconds, the minutes, every hour of the day, everything is associated with the four elements: fire, water, earth, air, also called

Order, Will, Wisdom, Earnestness. Everything radiates, communicates and stores according to our five components: feeling, sensing, thinking, speaking and acting. Our soul and physical body are oriented to the All.

All outer space radiates and is in movement and thus, also the human being. Our person belongs to the Earth and the Earth to the solar system, and our soul to the corresponding purification plane, which we ourselves determine every day through our five components. On the other hand, the soul's core of being belongs to the All-Being. Every soul has a so-called core of being. This is the essence of the Kingdom of God and thus, All-cosmic. The Kingdom of God has its eternal laws. It is the basic law of the love for God and neighbor.

People in the Spirit of God think further, for the messianic, sophianic age, the age of the lily has been announced.

The radiation of the Christ of God, together with the divine Wisdom, conveys to many people the certainty that a New Era is beginning, the age of the lily, the sovereign law of life, the love for God and neighbor.

People in this time live in the Spirit of God, who is the freedom—without priestly religion and without priestly guilds. Their role model is Jesus of Nazareth and the teaching of freedom in the Spirit, God, who is the freedom.

People of the New Era in the age of the lily are in communication with the All-Might and All-Wisdom of God, the omnipresent Being, which is the All-communication, the "being free" in the Spirit, God. Their prayer is communication, which means:

> Lift up the stone and focus your prayer on it, and you will gradually be certain that in

the depths, which is the All in all things, you will find the Spirit of God, the life.

Communicate with the stone and you experience God in you. Look at a flower, focus your prayer on it, until you notice that there is movement in you, then you experience God in you.

Look at an animal and focus on it, that is, focus your consciousness on it, be quiet and still, absorb the animal in you, and in your feelings, you experience the delicacy of this being, and you experience God.

Know that the All-communication is the core of being in your soul that is in eternal communication with the All-Wisdom, God.

Look at the crown of a tree and raise your prayer focus to it, which means: Concentrate on it and do not allow any side thoughts, then you notice that your prayers become ever deeper, and you recognize God in you.

All that is the beginning of the age of the lily, of freedom and unity, God, the life in all things.

Jesus of Nazareth taught us that the Kingdom of God is within, in you. That means that the core of being in the very basis of our soul is the essence of the Kingdom of God, it is the eternal law, the essence in all Being.

This statement—the core of being is the essence of the Kingdom of God, it is the eternal law, the All-Being—has deep and all-embracing significance.

Truly, we learn to live.
Truly, we will have an inkling of God, the All-Law of life, which is the love for God and neighbor. Let yourself be given a gift by the All-Life, which extends the lily to you, the All-Love of God, the love for neighbor.

Jesus, the Christ, sets cosmic signs. More and more human beings and souls are walking the path of freedom, of love for God and neighbor, for His coming is announced in the messianic, sophianic age of the lily, of the emerging purity of the human race.

Gabriele—Sophia

God-Father—
The Eternal Word

*God-Father,
the Eternal All-One,
Gave a Revelation in March 2019
through His Prophetess and Emissary
Gabriele*

The Messianic, Sophianic Age

God-Father—
The Eternal Word

And the word became flesh and still dwells among the people.
I, the I Am, Am the eternal word.

The Omega is spoken for this world.
I Am the eternal law, the Alpha, the origin of all true life, which is eternal.

On the cross, Jesus, the Christ, spoke the "It is finished." Indeed, He has accomplished it.

In the "It is finished," of My Son, of the Christ of God, is the proclamation: *"Come all to Me, the Christ of God, you, who labor and are heavy-laden—that is, who are caught up by the world—and follow Me, for I come soon."*

That is also the call of the divine Wisdom: Come to Him, to the Christ of God in you. He leads you to the eternal Father, who is in heaven.

The times of times contain the call of the Christ of God and of the divine Wisdom:
You ensouled human beings and you souls, follow the path to the true life, the path of peace, which is the primordial-eternal law, the path of the love for God and neighbor.

I Am the Father-Mother-God, the divine All-manifestation of the filiation attributes of Kindness, Love and Meekness—also called Patience, Love and Mercy—and I Am in the drawing and creating powers Order, Will, Wisdom and Earnestness.

The word of truth is also the word of the nation of children, of the sons and daughters of God, who spiritually personify the All-Life, the primordial-eternal law, which I Am.

The word of truth is also the essence in the soul of those who are still caught in human bodies and are waiting to see whether I truly Am the I Am.

I Am not the sign in those who lie in wait to see whether I give a sign of Myself—and this, if possible, in themselves or in the world. People with this attitude are like ashes in the wind, blown from one corner to the other, from one side of the street to the other.

I Am the primordial-eternal law and, as a Being of the Being, the divine embodiment, the divine manifestation, of the Father-Mother-God.

Before the primordial throne, before the Father-Mother-God, the eternal Being, are the seven princes with their duals. They are the four natures and the three filiation attributes. All seven basic powers are entity-powers, law-guardians of the Kingdom of God. Each dual pair, each princely pair, bears the regency of the corresponding basic power of law.

The seven basic powers form the unity of the Being, the spiritual basic law and the sequence of law of the love for God and neighbor. United, the seven basic powers, in them the three filiation attributes, are the primordial Creator-power in the stream of creation, the Being. The essence of every basic power is contained in each of the others.

The Sanctum of the Being is the primordial Creator-power, the flowing All-Law, the inexhaustible, giving Light-Ether.

Seven times seven eons, mighty All-orbits, move around the Sanctum, also called the primordial clockwork or Primordial Central Sun, with its seven prism suns. The sons and daughters of God live and work in the seven times seven courses of eons. They constitute countless divine families and the corresponding clans. They are all at home in the All-Being, the law of life.

I Am the primordial God, also called the Father-Mother-Being. My sons and daughters are heirs to the Being. They are compressed

All-law, beings of the Being, and form the unity, the Being in the Being, the Kingdom of God. The eternal homeland, the primordial-eternal Being, is embedded in noble gardens. In the gardens of the All-life are the fine-material buildings of the divine families.

The Being in the Being is the insurmountable law of the primordial-eternal love for God and neighbor. The primordial Being can be compared to a fine-material all-irradiated crystal. The primordial Being is the eternal life, which began with the primordial creation, with the "Let there be," which is the unity, the love for God and neighbor.

From the love for God and neighbor, the "Let there be," emerged the nation of children of which I, who I Am, have already made known several times, giving the people an understanding of the life of the Being, through the word of the heralds of God, through the prophets and prophetesses.

Again and again I, who I Am, spoke into My emissaries, into incarnated sons and daughters.

I, who I Am, call the primordial-eternal word through the mouth of prophets the "word that became flesh." That is also how it is in this cosmic time. My word became flesh once more, and still dwells among the people.

Hear My words and heed their content, for I Am the primordial-eternal law, the I Am, the Father-Mother-God of My children.

In the Kingdom of God, in the mighty All-Father's house of My children, My sons and daughters, a small evil took place—through the first act of creation of the "Let there be"—which threatened to escalate. Revealed in a general way, some of My sons and daughters became lukewarm and believed the false word, that the Kingdom of God of the love for God and neighbor should be given a different structure. They began to rebel against the All-law of unity and freedom and wanted to prove that they could do better than the primordial creation, the forces of drawing and creating, of which the three filiation attributes are a part.

All in all, the seven primordial forces of drawing and creating are also their seven-dimensional heritage, which they lived and ultimately possess since the primordial creation of Being. The primordial-eternal law, which is unity, the same as freedom, enabled them to produce evidence that their desire for drawing and creating would bear fruit. The I Am who I Am and the law-guardians of the love for God and neighbor, the seven princes, gave them a mighty quantum of spiritual, primordial-atomic Light-Ether to take with them, so that they themselves be able to draw and create. The quantum of Light-Ether determined a certain time in the times. Therefore, it is a loan from the eternal Being.

The Fall-system has often been reported about, also through My Son, the Christ of God, once in Jesus of Nazareth. The renewed explanations to the Fall event are important in order to understand that the "It is finished" of My Son, the Co-Regent of the Kingdom of God, is significant, because through it, the homebringing of willing sons and daughters was initiated and thus, Redemption from bondage to the Fall-realm. The end of the Fall was thus accomplished in the "It is finished." It is done.

The victory of the Co-Regent of the Kingdom of God and the victory of the divine Wisdom, of the primordial Wisdom in Me, were the prerequisites for leading back the sons and daughters of God and for the transformation of density, of matter.

The Fall yesterday and today.

I will call the times of times the yesterday and the today, for I Am the Eternal and the Eternity.

Yesterday, the rebellion against Me, who I Am, began, and thus, against the Kingdom of God, which is the homeland of the children of God, of My sons and daughters. My rebellious sons and daughters accepted from Me the quantum power of spiritual-atomic Light-Ether without hesitation—a loan, in order to prove their mastery.

That is how it was yesterday. First of all, they created a Wall of Light, through which they completely distanced themselves from the Kingdom of God, their homeland, and from Me, the Father-Mother-God.

What is it like today? Walls upon walls, fences upon fences, each one thinking he is greater than the other. The divisiveness of yesterday is also the separation of today.

My sons and daughters, during your long cosmic wanderings, have you thought about the fact that it is merely sounds of differing nuances that come out of a mouth? You have made words from this mesh of sounds, in order to communicate with each other to some extent. If words or sentences have no content that expresses what you want to say to your neighbor, then you talk past one another. Why? Because unfilled words are merely hollow words. From this, what first develop are sparring matches, then, dissension, all the way to war, that is, fratricide.

What do you human beings want?

The majority of people, regardless on which continent the loner ekes out his existence, hardly notices that in the times of times they move in a so-called ink, with which the Omega has long since been written for this world and for the so-called material cosmos, and beyond that, for other finer-material cosmoses, in which the souls live, ultimately, you, too, once you are disincarnate—for I, who I Am, Am the eternal life.

With their quarreling, the Fall-sons and Fall-daughters of yesterday formed religions. Human gods were chosen as gods of religions, who provide their service to their believers to this day.

Everything is a spectacle of the Fall and has nothing in common with the All-Being, the All-One, who I Am.

The primordial-eternal law, the love for God and neighbor, is the unity and the peace, the beauty of the eternal homeland and the loyalty to the eternal law of life, which I Am.

Your Fall-numbers—regardless of what you call them—are truly Fall-oriented numbers. Within, they contain the deterioration. Without thinking about what this means, each one of you walks into the trap yourselves, for your law of "divide, bind, and rule" is the mantrap that initiates the crash of your world theater.

Verily, I, who I Am, the primordial-eternal Love and the primordial-eternal Wisdom—I do not leave you. With the primordial law of love and love of neighbor, I go after you and fetch you home, you, who wade in the swamp of your ink.

In all the times of times, I, who I Am, went after you through prophets and prophetesses and through many who were turned to Me. I went after you through My first Son in Jesus of Nazareth. I go after you through My first daughter, who is the dual of the Cherub of My primordial Wisdom.

The supporting pair of the divine Wisdom, of the primordial Wisdom, has obligated itself to carry out with My Son, the Christ of God, the homebringing of My sons and daughters, for the Omega is spoken.

As already revealed, all prophets and prophetesses of God have spoken the word, the I Am. That means that beings of light took on flesh.

They incorporated themselves into human bodies, to show their brothers and sisters the path back into the eternal Father's house, into the primordial-eternal law, which is eternal Love.

In this most recent time, it is once again: *"And the word became flesh and dwells among the people."* My word is the word of revelation through a human being, through whom I, the I Am the I Am, reveal Myself to the people, just as at all times through the heralds of God, the prophets of God.

People of past times did not want to hear My word, the eternal word, the I Am.

What is it like in the present time? Many people of the present time are still dependent on religion, and are more attached to the belief in gods than to the Free Spirit, God, who does not demand anything of them, who exclusively taught and teaches through His heralds, the path of the commandments through Moses, which are the steps of the law to life. The path to the true life is merely shown, but not enforced.

The Christ of God, incarnated in Jesus of Nazareth, My first-beheld and spiritually firstborn Son, the Co-Regent of the eternal Kingdom of Peace, of unity, of the love for God and neighbor, became the sacrifice on the cross, in order to save the souls through the Redeemer-light, which He released from His divine heritage, thus accomplishing Redemption.

My primordial-eternal word continued without interruption, and that, from herald of God to herald of God, and through countless God-conscious men and women, as well.

At all times, the eternal word, the I Am, revealed itself through the mouth of prophets. Just as once—through the prophets and prophetesses of God and through many enlightened men and women, and not lastly, through Jesus of Nazareth, the incarnated Christ—I, who I Am, reveal Myself again through a human being, and that, today, and not yesterday.

The chaos of energy of My sons and daughters sank ever deeper and has now reached a depth that is critical. Once again, it needs a further feat by My Son, the Christ of God, and by the divine Wisdom.

The yesterday is also the today, yet not the tomorrow. Since the times of times are approaching the end, I reveal Myself anew, in order to once more call My sons and daughters. Many people still cling to the hollow words of the delegates of religion, of priests and pastors, and seek protection with a God who does not exist in the religious presentations.

When will My sons and daughters grasp that they are ensouled human beings, that is, that they have a soul, in which is the compressed law of the eternal Being, the essence of the Kingdom of God, the core of being, which has within the sonship and daughtership of God? It is a true eternal heritage, the eternal Being, the elixir of life of the seven basic powers.

I who I Am, want to again reveal today, that is, in the present time, about the import of My Son's sacrifice on the cross—not what those in religious robes have served up to the majority of the people.

My first-beheld and spiritually created Son, the Co-Regent of the Kingdom of God, incarnated, that is, became a human being—Jesus of Nazareth. He, the carpenter, the son of the carpenter Joseph, was now the prophet Jesus of Nazareth.

Jesus of Nazareth, the carpenter, taught the law of heaven and healed with the law of heaven. At the end of His time on Earth, He fared much the same as many messengers of God. As at all times in the times, the majority of the people listened to the guilds of priests and the members of religions such as emperors, kings, princes and their servants.

Right into the present time, the call of the incited people resounds: "Kill Him, Jesus of Nazareth, burn those who follow Him, or hang them." The same call applied to many prophets and prophetesses right into the present time.

Jesus of Nazareth walked the way of the cross, without rebelling against His enemies, accompanied by the Cherubim and Seraphim and, in His heart, by the Spirit, His Father, who is the life in all things, the I Am the I Am, the Father-Mother-God of all My children.

All the faithful men and women bore a similar yoke, the martyrdom, which was imposed on them. By whom? By the system from below.

Through torture and pain upon pain, the Baalistic system wanted to press them into striking back and ultimately commit fratricide and become disloyal to the God of love. That would have been the defeat in the struggle, in order to then ascribe to Me, the I Am, the love for God and neighbor, what is still the sign in this world today—fratricide.

The sacrifice on the cross of Jesus of Nazareth was not an expiatory sacrifice for the fallen ones, but the beginning of the homebringing of the sons and daughters of God and the repudiation of the desire of the Fall-tirades to dissolve creation, the Being.

With the analogous words of Jesus of Nazareth, *"It is finished,"* and with the surrender of His divine being to the Spirit of His eternal Father, to the I Am the I Am, the Co-Regent of the Kingdom of God bestowed a part of His heavenly heritage on all souls and ensouled human beings. The divine part-heritage transferred to each soul the energetic spark, which is protection, a hold and guidance, also for the ensouled human beings.

His divine, released part-heritage is also called the Redeemer-spark. Through His "It is finished," with which He simultaneously placed His Spirit, His eternal Oneness with Me, the Father-Mother-God, into the cosmic Being, the Earth trembled with joy, for it is a living organism that is calling for liberation and for the return of the life forms of the nature kingdoms. The call for liberation also rings out in the finer-material cosmoses, which in the times of times became the purification planes of the souls.

After it was "accomplished," My Son, once in Jesus of Nazareth, returned to the eternal Father, who I Am, to the law of love for God and neighbor.

esterday, the Alpha, today, the Omega.

Despite all that, a review for people who turn to the New Era.

After Jesus of Nazareth, early Christianity emerged. More and more communities of brothers and sisters joined together to ignite the Christ-spark more and more through the heavenly teachings that Jesus of Nazareth had taught the people and which He also had personified as Jesus of Nazareth.

What happened?

The father from below, who was a liar from the beginning, as Jesus of Nazareth called him, built up his might, his system, just as fraudulent as he simply is, under the name of Jesus of Nazareth, in order to deceive his believers, and does not hesitate to abuse the law of love for God and neighbor.

The Baal system, the father from below, builds his law of bondage, selfishness and self-love on the law of freedom, of love for God and neighbor. Many communities, which wanted to live the law of love for God and neighbor, fell victim to the "power trip" of church and state under the Baal system.

Religions, which bear within the driving force of power to eradicate everything that does not correspond to their guidelines, infiltrate and often appropriate the authority of the state.

Into the present time, followers of the teachings of Jesus of Nazareth are persecuted by the system of "divide, bind and rule."

To this day, the blatancy of this Baalistic system is in the use of the name of the eternal Being, God, and that, without scruples. This principle has nothing in common with the One God, the Father-Mother-God, the Creator of the Being, who I Am.

My Word became flesh by way of the incarnation of beings faithful to God, of prophets and prophetesses of God, through whom I spoke the word of eternity, the I Am, and through My Son, the Co-Regent of the Kingdom of God, once in the human being Jesus of Nazareth. Everything else is wastage, theft of the name Jesus of Nazareth.

May it be repeated:
The "It is finished" is accomplished, and the Redeemer-spark is in the core of being of every soul.

After the first feat, "It is finished," followed the second step to the second feat. The second step was initiated in the Kingdom of God. My Son, once in Jesus of Nazareth, and the Cherubim, activated the second step, the second feat.

The point is not to destroy the world, but to fetch home and to guide home anyone who lets himself be guided by the primordial Love, which I Am. The primordial law, the primordial Love, which I Am, calls His sons and daughters, to gradually accept their normality, which lies in their spiritual heritage to be the equality, the freedom, the unity, the brotherliness, that is, brotherli-sisterliness, as they were beheld and created by Me, the I Am, the primordial Love, the primordial law of love for God and neighbor.

Since it is as it is, after the first step, the "It is finished," the supporting pair of My divine Wisdom, the primordial Wisdom in the primordial Love, which I Am, accepted the second step. The Cherub and the Seraph of Wisdom, My third basic power before My throne, accepted the second feat, the second step.

For better understanding:

The Wisdom of God in Me, who I Am, is the work of the deed in the Kingdom of God, the implementing basic law for the All-life. And in the divine-atomic All-structuring of the Being, the primordial Love and primordial Wisdom are the driving force of the divine-atomic Light-Ether, the giving and receiving principle, the Being. The All-Being is the omnipresent life, the All-Love.

May it be repeated: After Jesus of Nazareth, communities arose with corresponding group names that differed from time to time and that upheld the teachings of Jesus of Nazareth, the law of love and faithfulness to the teachings of Jesus, the Christ, and lived accordingly. Soon the religious guild, the Baal system with its horrible, brutal and bestial system of extermination, mostly in connection with the respective state organ, began to carry out its Baalistic nefarious deeds.

The part-ray of the divine Wisdom, the Seraph, was also in the earthly garment in the various early Christian communities, in order to help with the spiritual development of a higher ethics and morals that is lived, in the following of Jesus of Nazareth. From the Kingdom of God, the Cherub of divine Wisdom accompanied his spiritual dual on the Earth, to provide support and help together with brothers and sisters who wanted to follow the teachings of Jesus of Nazareth.

During the centuries since Jesus of Nazareth, the Seraph of divine Wisdom incarnated again and again, and, as a human being among human beings, taught how to live the law of God. As a human being, who went over the Earth with different names from incarnation to incarnation, she fared the same as all her brothers and sisters, who remained faithful to the teachings of Jesus of Nazareth—the terrible persecution through tirades of lies, slander and character assassination all the way to the extermination of the many early Christian communities, which the Moloch mercilessly eradicated, as at all times.

May it be repeated for understanding: With her spirit-dual, the Cherub of divine Wisdom, the incarnated Seraph of divine Wisdom assumed, with the Christ of God, the divine mission to call all willing sons and daughters of God and to lead the people on the path of the Christ of God.

The Cherub of the third basic power before My Throne, who accompanied his spirit-dual, had to look on as brothers and sisters, men and women, were bestially tortured and executed, often with the cross of agony with corpus before their eyes and under the abuse of the name of the Prince of Peace, Jesus of Nazareth. Into the present time, the corpus on the cross, the so-called crucifix, is of importance to the religious Baal system and its appendage, the state.

Why is that so?

The second announced step followed, that included a further feat.

Once again, the part-ray, the Seraph of divine Wisdom, incarnated, to set with her spirit-dual from the Sanctum of the Being, the last feat into motion, the homebringing of the willing sons and daughters of God. This divine mission also includes laying the cornerstone for building New Jerusalem, for the New Era.

In the present time, in the year in which conflicts flared up again according to the Fall-principle "divide, bind and rule," a child came into being, in it, again, the Seraph of divine Wisdom.

The child matured into a woman and took part in the life on Earth. In the middle of her lifetime, her spirit-dual, the Cherub of My Wisdom, made himself known, introducing himself as her spiritual teacher, who should train her on My behalf, in order to serve Me as prophetess and emissary of the Kingdom of God.

After a short period of orientation, the person with the present name Gabriele answered the request from the Kingdom of God in the affirmative. It was not difficult for the teacher, the Cherub of My Wisdom, to prepare the human being, Gabriele, for the divine prophetic word, since the inner being in the person is, on the one hand, his dual, the Seraph of Wisdom, and on the other hand, the Seraph had several incarnations behind her—not to say, many.

During the various incarnations, her soul, today, in the human being Gabriele, came to know the people, for example, what the sound of a person's words reveals, what his clothing reveals, the movements of his body, also his food, the preparation of his food and way of eating.

Everything is energy, and everything sends. The person himself is a sender and receiver. In the former existences of the Seraph, the human being learned to perceive the tone and sound of the various human bodies, and thus behave accordingly. Many of these imprints in her soul were used by the Cherub of My Wisdom to likewise train her as a teaching prophetess.

Gabriele's path as a prophet once again became the eternal word made flesh, the I Am the I Am. Gabriele, the prophetess of God, traveled to many places, cities, countries and continents to give My eternal word, the I Am. The Cherub of My Wisdom, who accompanied My prophetess from the eternal Being, took from her soul and—as was his spiritual mission—from the prism suns of the seven law powers and from the atmospheric Christ-chronicle the eternal word, which had been revealed over the millennia by the messengers of God.

The Cherub also had the eternal word through Jesus of Nazareth revealed again, just as I, the I Am, once announced it through the prophet Isaiah: *"My word does not return empty to Me."* It has returned and has again become flesh. What I, who I Am, once announced through the prophet Isaiah, has been accomplished by the Cherub of My Wisdom, and that, together with his Seraph in the earthly garment, My prophetess of the present time.

In the hearts of many Original Christians worldwide and in faithful God-seekers a New Era is dawning:

It is the Era of the Christ of God, the Messianic, Sophianic Age of the Lily, of freedom, love and unity in Me, the Father-Mother-God, and the Christ of God, who is the way to Me, to the I Am who I Am, to the law of peace, of the love for God and neighbor.

Very gradually, the fetters of the "divide, bind and rule" system, will also break, in which lie the eradication instructions of the religious doctrine, the binding anchor between state and church against the teachings of Jesus of Nazareth, against the Christ of God and against the followers of Jesus of Nazareth.

The New Era includes building New Jerusalem for the Kingdom of Peace of Jesus Christ. It will still take time, for I Am the peace. I do not fight with the weapons of state and church. My fight is the struggle for all My sons and daughters, for every being of the Being, no matter how much it is still entangled and bound in the world. So it was at all times, so it is also in the present time. My prophets and prophetesses, the messengers of God, did not fight with the weapons of state and church. Their sign of victory is valid into the present time; it is the eternal law, the love for God and neighbor. That is the feature of all the messengers of God and also the seal of the bringing and leading home of My sons and daughters.

I Am who I Am, the Father-Mother-God of all My children. I Am the I Am, the primordial-eternal law of love for God and neighbor.

In this consciousness of love for God and neighbor, the memorial site stands as a monument to the sacrifice on the cross of Redemption.

In this consciousness of the love for God and neighbor, *the Tent of God for All the Nations of this Earth, the Ark of the Covenant of the Free Spirit*, God, who I Am, and My eternal word that is spoken for many generations, stands.

Come all to your Redeemer, the Christ of God, for He is the way to Me, the Father-Mother-God. I Am the life of the Being.

Every soul and every ensouled human being is free to take this path. When he walks it, how he walks it, is free for every soul and every ensouled human being, but no one can avoid following the path with the Christ of God, for He is the path to life. He is the Risen One in every soul and thus, the way into the Kingdom of God, into the eternal Father's house.

The victory of the Christ of God
and of the divine Wisdom in Me
is the it is finished and
it is accomplished.

It is done, by Jesus, the Christ,
and the divine Wisdom.

The Fall-system,
the system of "divide, bind and rule,"
is defeated.

I Am who I Am,
the eternal Love, the Being.